Warren G. *Harding*

Warren G. *Harding*

Our Twenty-Ninth President

By Gerry and Janet Souter

SPIRIT
of America™

The Child's World®, Inc.
Chanhassen, Minnesota

7

WARREN G. *Harding*

Published in the United States of America by The Child's World®, Inc.
PO Box 326 • Chanhassen, MN 55317-0326 • 800-599-READ • www.childsworld.com

Acknowledgments
The Creative Spark: Mary Francis-DeMarois, Project Director; Elizabeth Sirimarco Budd, Series Editor; Robert Court, Design and Art Direction; Janine Graham, Page Layout; Jennifer Moyers, Production

The Child's World®, Inc.: Mary Berendes, Publishing Director; Red Line Editorial, Fact Research; Cindy Klingel, Curriculum Advisor; Robert Noyed, Historical Advisor

Photos
Cover: White House Collection, courtesy White House Historical Association; Bettmann/Corbis: 25, 26; Corbis: 20, 24; Library of Congress: 6, 13, 19, 22, 23, 28, 29, 30, 31, 33, 34; Courtesy of the Ohio Historical Society: 7, 8, 10, 12, 15, 18, 21, 35

Registration
The Child's World®, Inc., Spirit of America™, and their associated logos are the sole property and registered trademarks of The Child's World®, Inc.

Library of Congress Cataloging-in-Publication Data
Souter, Gerry.
    Warren G. Harding : our twenty-ninth president / by Gerry and Janet Souter.
        p. cm.
    Includes bibliographical references and index.
    ISBN 1-56766-839-9 (alk. paper : lib. bdg.)
    1. Harding, Warren G. (Warren Gamaliel), 1865–1923—Juvenile literature. 2. Presidents—United States—Biography—Juvenile literature. [1. Harding, Warren G. (Warren Gamaliel), 1865–1923.
2. Presidents.] I. Souter, Janet, 1940– II. Title.
    E786 S68 2001
    973.91'4'092—dc21

                                                            00-010548

15   19   33

Contents

Chapter ONE   *Born to Succeed*   6

Chapter TWO   *Warren and His Duchess*   12

Chapter THREE *A Difficult Presidency*   20

Chapter FOUR   *Journey to Disaster*   30

                 Time Line   36

                 Glossary Terms   38

                 Our Presidents   42

                 Presidential Facts   46

                 For Further Information   47

                 Index   48

Born to Succeed

Warren Harding became the 29th president in 1921, although many believed he was not cut out for such a great responsibility. One politician of the day said Harding's only qualification was that "he looked like a president."

THE CIVIL WAR HAD JUST ENDED WHEN Phoebe Dickerson Harding delivered her first-born child at the Harding farm in Corsica, Ohio. (Today Corsica is called Blooming Grove.) The date was November 2, 1865, and Phoebe and her husband named their child Warren Gamaliel Bancroft Winnipeg Harding. He would be the first of their eight children.

Warren's father, George Tryon Harding, was a doctor. Money was often hard to come by in America's farming communities, so people often traded goods and services with each other. The people of Corsica knew George Harding was willing to trade. In exchange for his medical services, he might accept a bag of seed instead of money. Then he might trade that seed for a shovel at the general store.

Phoebe Harding was always busy with farm chores, but she found time to begin Warren's education while he was still quite young. She was a religious woman and read the Bible to her son. She also taught him poems. Warren was a bright child and could read by age four.

By the time he was a teenager, Warren was tall and handsome. He was also muscular from working on his father's farm. His many friends enjoyed his company, but Warren was also independent. He liked to spend time by himself. In addition to working on his father's farm, young Warren helped build fences for his neighbors. He also worked for the Toledo & Ohio Railroad, helping to lay track.

George Harding wanted to help his son in any way he could. He gave Warren a small piece of land to farm. Warren could sell his

Warren, at age six, is shown here with two of his sisters. Warren could read by the time he was four years old, but his education was minimal. He was not a great student, and his grades were never among the best in his class.

crops to earn extra money. Then George Harding became part owner of a newspaper. Warren took a job at the paper as the "printer's devil." This meant he did odd jobs around the office. He swept up, cleaned ink off the print machines, ran errands, and learned about the business of running a small weekly newspaper.

Even with his busy work schedule, Warren liked to have a good time. He enjoyed music and learned to play a horn. Then he and his friends started a band. Warren's outgoing nature and good looks made him popular. The band allowed him to travel throughout the county, making more friends along the way.

In 1879, at age 14, Warren entered tiny Ohio Central College to study with its faculty of 12 instructors. He became the editor of the school newspaper, called the *Ohio Central College Journal of Knowledge and Josh.* (Josh is another word for "joke.") This gave Warren the chance to have his writing published for the first time. In the summer, he painted barns for $25 each, including the paint. He used the money to help pay his **tuition.** It seemed like everything was going well for hardworking Warren Harding. His life was on the right track.

Still a teenager, Warren graduated from college and then passed the Ohio State teaching exam. He tried teaching but didn't like it. Then he tried selling insurance, but he disliked that as well. When his family moved to Marion, Ohio, in 1882, Warren took a job with the *Marion Democratic Mirror* newspaper as a writer—and a floor sweeper.

Unfortunately, Warren's career at the *Mirror* was brief. The Hardings were **Republicans,** and the editor at the newspaper was a staunch **Democrat.** People from the two **political parties** often had differences of opinion. In 1884, the Republicans **nominated** James G. Blaine as their presidential **candidate.** He ran against the Democratic candidate, Grover Cleveland. Warren went to a political **rally** for Blaine and returned to work wearing a paper hat with a Blaine ribbon attached. The editor fired him on the spot.

▸ In addition to being a **homeopathic** doctor, George Harding taught himself veterinary medicine.

Warren graduated from Ohio Central College when he was just 16 years old. He then tried his hand at teaching. Eventually, he decided to pursue a career in journalism.

Warren was not out of the newspaper business for long. Two of his friends heard that a small newspaper business in Marion was for sale. They suggested that the three of them pool their money and buy it for $300. Warren had always liked **journalism.** He put in his share of the money and became part owner of the newspaper at age 19.

Over the next five years, Warren Harding learned every part of the newspaper business, from setting type to deciding what stories the newspaper would print. Later he became the sole owner of the *Marion Star.* He became an important member of the community, respected by the townspeople. He established a unique **creed** for his paper that told its employees what was expected of them. Harding wanted to run his paper with honesty and integrity. He hated **sensational** articles that lured readers with stories of crime, tragedy, and misfortune. Part of his creed stated: "There's good in everybody. Bring out the good in everybody, and never needlessly hurt the feelings of anybody."

WARREN HARDING CREATED AND POSTED THIS SET
of rules for his *Star* employees to follow as they wrote
their news stories. The following are some of his ideas
about how journalists should do their work.

The Star Office Creed

- Remember there are two sides to every question. Get both.

- Be truthful.

- Get the facts. Mistakes are inevitable, but strive for accuracy. I would rather have one story exactly right then a hundred half wrong.

- Be decent. Be fair. Be generous.

- Boost—don't knock. There's good in everybody. Bring out the good in everybody, and never needlessly hurt the feelings of anybody.

- In reporting a political gathering, get the facts; tell the story as it is, not as you would like to have it.

- Treat all parties alike. If there is any politics to be played, we will play it in our editorial columns.

- Treat all religious matters reverently.

- If it can possibly be avoided, never bring ignominy to an innocent woman or child in telling the misdeeds or misfortune of a relative. Don't wait to be asked, but do it without asking.

- And, above all, be clean. Never let a dirty word or suggestive story get into type.

I want this paper so conducted that it can go into any home without destroying the innocence of a child.

Warren G. Harding
Editor & Publisher of the *Marion Star*

Chapter TWO

Warren and His Duchess

Warren Harding became well known in his community as the owner of the Marion Star. *His good looks and charm gained him many admirers.*

SOME PEOPLE SAY WARREN HARDING MET HIS future wife, Florence Kling De Wolfe, at the town's roller-skating rink. Others remembered that Florence first saw Warren standing on a street corner. She was so impressed by the handsome newspaperman, she asked a friend to find a way to introduce them. Others say they met when Florence was teaching Warren's younger sister to play piano.

Florence's father, Amos Kling, was the richest man in town. Mr. Kling hoped she would one day marry a nice young man who would take over his successful businesses. Instead, Florence had an unhappy first marriage that ended in divorce. Her father disapproved of the relationship from the start. After the divorce, he was not very helpful to her.

Florence wasn't pretty or gentle, as women were supposed to be in those days. Instead, she was bright, independent, and full of **ambition.** Since her father wouldn't help her, she decided to earn money by teaching piano. Among her students was one of Warren's younger sisters. Florence loved the Harding family. The house was filled with laughter and warmth. Then she met Warren, who was five years younger than she was. Florence fell in love.

Warren was charming and generous, and his good looks won admirers wherever he went. He had many girlfriends, but Warren noticed something special about Florence. He was pleased that the daughter of Marion's wealthiest citizen liked him. She was bright and interested in learning about his business. He still wasn't ready to give up his other girlfriends, but Florence waited patiently. Finally, Warren asked her to marry him. They were married on July 8, 1891.

Florence Kling Harding (shown here after she became the first lady) played an important role in her husband's career. She helped his newspaper run smoothly and later encouraged him to enter politics.

Florence Harding's father didn't approve of his daughter's new husband. He tried to ruin the *Marion Star* by scaring away its advertisers. He told nasty stories about the Harding family to anyone who would listen. Mrs. Harding did not give up on her husband. If anything, she became more committed to his success.

Shortly after they were married, Mrs. Harding went to work at the *Star*. She planned to help out for just a few days but ended up working there for 14 years. She took over the **circulation** department. She made sure that customers paid for their subscriptions and that newsboys delivered the papers on time. She also took over the advertising department. The Hardings turned the paper into one of most successful in the state.

Warren Harding admired his wife for her education and her strength. He also respected her good business sense. He called her his "Duchess." Warren now concentrated on writing **editorials** for the paper. The *Marion Star* thrived and soon became the Harding Publishing Company.

Florence Harding helped manage business affairs for the Marion Star. *This allowed her husband to concentrate on journalism. He worked hard to give his newspaper a positive image.*

Seven years after their marriage, the "Duchess" and several of their friends suggested that Harding run for a seat in the Ohio State Senate. Although Warren was sure he wasn't cut out for **politics,** Mrs. Harding and their friends would not give up. Harding was elected to the senate in 1898 when he was only 33 years old.

Harding carried his newspaper's creed into politics. He believed there was good in everybody and immediately won a reputation as an honest man. He was a "team player" who always went along with the Republican Party **policies.** When there were disagreements, people counted on Harding to restore peace. Even the Democrats liked him, and they were his party's opponents.

Harding's popularity kept him at the center of the Republican Party. In 1903,

Myron T. Herrick became the governor of Ohio. For his party loyalty, Harding was rewarded with the job of lieutenant governor. This sent him to the state capital, Columbus. His term ended in 1905, and the Hardings returned to Marion. In 1910, the Republicans chose Harding as their candidate for governor, a race that he lost. Harding was disappointed and vowed never to run for another office. It would not take long for him to break this vow.

The Republicans knew Harding was loyal to the party and asked him to run for the U.S. Senate. At first, he refused. But once again, his wife and their political friends changed his mind. After winning the election in 1914, the Hardings moved to Washington, D.C. Florence Harding was thrilled by her new position as the wife of a U.S. senator. Soon they were friends with some of the wealthiest and most important citizens in the nation's capital.

Harding plunged into his work with enthusiasm. When he wasn't on the floor of the Senate, he enjoyed poker parties with old friends from Ohio and new friends he met in

Washington. Mrs. Harding did not like to gamble, so she acted as the hostess.

One of his fellow senators said that Harding loved being a senator, but he didn't like all the work and responsibility that went with it. Harding proposed 132 **bills** in his six-year career, but few were of any great importance. Still, he became a notable figure in the Republican Party.

President Woodrow Wilson was too ill in 1920 to seek another term, so the Democrats nominated James Cox. The Republican Party was split between two candidates, General Leonard Wood and Frank O. Lowden. Ohio Republicans named Harding as a candidate as well, but no one expected him to win the nomination. Harding himself wasn't interested in running for president. "The only thing I really worry about," he said, "is that I might be nominated."

That summer, the Republican Party held its national **convention** in Chicago. It took place during one of the worst heat waves in the city's history. Unfortunately, the party couldn't decide between the two favorite candi-dates. Both of them refused to withdraw from the race. The temperature at the convention hall reached 106 degrees. The **delegates** were ready to make a decision and go home.

A group of Republican Party leaders gathered at the Blackstone Hotel to solve the problem. The choice that finally came from the smoke-filled room was Warren Harding. One senator called him "the best of the second-raters." If he wasn't the party's first choice, he was the best of their second choices.

Harding accepted their decision, saying, "The fates ... have drawn me into the presidential race." At first, Mrs. Harding wasn't excited about the prospect. By this time, both the Hardings had serious health problems. She worried that the demands of the presidency would be too much for them. Still, she mustered up the enthusiasm to help her husband **campaign** for office.

Harding accepts his party's nomination at the 1920 Republican Party National Convention.

FROM THE BEGINNING OF U.S. HISTORY UNTIL 1920, WOMEN WERE NOT allowed to vote in elections. The right to vote is called suffrage, and women began fighting for this right in the mid-19th century. Women struggling to win the vote became known as suffragettes.

The suffragettes struggled for more than half a century to achieve their goal. Florence Harding had always supported this quest. She saw to it that her husband supported it, too. In 1920—just in time for Warren Harding's presidential campaign—the 19th Amendment was passed. American women could cast their ballots for the first time. This added 25 million new voters to the population.

Both Republicans and Democrats wanted to win women's votes. During the presidential campaign of 1920, Mrs. Harding was proof of how women could play important roles in business and politics. Many American women respected her ambition and drive. Thanks in large part to her, Warren Harding won a large majority of women's votes.

Chapter THREE

A Difficult Presidency

"I expect it is very possible," said Harding, "that I would make as good a president as a great many men who are talked of for that position."

INSTEAD OF TOURING THE COUNTRY TO GET votes, Harding used his home in Marion as the campaign headquarters. The American people came to him. Harding called this the "front-porch campaign." Movie stars and entertainers visited the Harding home, as did politicians and business leaders. Marching bands and throngs of ordinary citizens arrived by bus and train from across the country.

The theme of Harding's campaign was "Return to Normalcy." President Wilson had become known as a cold intellectual who didn't care about the American people. He had also been very ill during his last year in office, which worried many citizens. The Hardings convinced voters that they were ordinary people, just like other Americans.

People wanted to forget about the hardships of World War I (which had ended in 1918) and of Wilson's presidency. They wanted a change of leadership. Harding won a **landslide** victory, becoming the 29th president of the United States.

The American people loved the small-town businessman who had become president. In fact, during his term, he was one of the most popular presidents in history. But Harding

Harding used his skill as a speaker during his front-porch campaign. He promised to help America return to "normalcy," the good old days before World War I and Wilson's presidency.

21

President Harding (second from left) was the first president to ride to his inauguration in a motorcar instead of a horse-drawn carriage. He is shown here with Woodrow Wilson on Inauguration Day.

Interesting Facts

▸ Following World War I, President Wilson proposed a League of Nations, an earlier version of today's United Nations. The League was accepted by all the European powers in 1919, but Republican politicians worked to keep the United States out of it. One month after becoming president, Harding announced that he would not support U.S. membership in the League of Nations.

was aware of his limitations. He surrounded himself with the "best minds" for his **cabinet.** Among these men was a well-known judge named Charles Evans Hughes, Harding's secretary of state. Hughes was in charge of the country's relations with other countries. Future president Herbert Hoover was the secretary of commerce, in charge of business affairs. Financial wizard Andrew Mellon became the secretary of the **treasury.** He was in charge of the government's money.

Unfortunately, Harding gave other important positions to friends without such strong backgrounds. He named Albert Fall as his

secretary of the interior. He named his campaign manager, Harry Daugherty, the **attorney general.** Harding chose another friend, Charles Forbes, to head the Veteran's **Bureau.** He would regret these choices later.

President Harding worked hard at his job. He arrived at his desk at 8 o'clock every morning, and he often stayed until midnight. But being the president was a difficult job. Harding began to fear that he could not live up to such responsibility. "I am just beginning to realize what a job I have taken over," said Harding. "God help me, for I need it."

Calvin Coolidge (right) was Harding's vice president. Here the Hardings and the Coolidges pose for a portrait after Harding's inauguration.

The president did have his successes. He proposed a new government office called the Bureau of the Budget. This bureau was in charge of creating the first formal budget for government spending. Just like a family, the government cannot spend more money than it has. It needs to carefully plan how it will spend its money. Such a plan is called a budget.

Before the new bureau was created, each department in the government handled its

One positive force during Harding's term was the widespread use of new technology, such as the telephone, that made it easier for world leaders to communicate with each other. He is shown here (fifth from left) in 1921 opening telephone communication with Cuba.

own budget. This often resulted in over-spending. Creating the bureau saved money. In fact, it helped bring about the country's first balanced budget. This meant it was the first time the government did not spend more money than it had.

Harding improved relationships with nations that had been enemies of the United States during World War I. He also recognized that the automobile would change the world in the coming years, so he supported the construction of highways around the country. He lowered taxes, pleasing the American people.

President Harding loved sports, including fishing, boxing, golf, and baseball. He followed baseball scores and invited the great Babe Ruth (shown here shaking hands with the president) to the White House on many occasions.

25

Harding always enjoyed a good round of golf. As his political life grew more stressful, sports were a way for him to relax.

In 1921, Harding proposed the Washington Conference for the Limitation of **Armament.** This meeting was meant to control the amount of weapons (arms) that countries could keep. The United States, Great Britain, Japan, France, and Italy all agreed to limit the size of their military forces. Harding delivered the opening speech by remembering the brutality of World War I: "How can humanity justify, or God forgive? ... Our hundreds of millions [of people] frankly want less of armament and none of war."

Harding's social life did not change very much after he became president. Twice-weekly poker parties for Harding's pals were held on the second floor of the White House. He also played golf whenever he could. Mrs. Harding opened the White House for parties of her own. In fact, she opened the gates to the president's gardens so that the public could wander freely around the grounds. She believed the White House belonged to all Americans, not just the president and his family.

By 1922, Harding's presidency seemed to be going well. But it all soon began to collapse. Both Harding and his wife were still troubled by health problems. To make matters worse, **corruption** among Harding's "friends" was threatening to destroy his presidency.

One of the worst **scandals** involved Albert Fall, the secretary of the interior. He was caught selling the rights to drill for oil on government lands to private oil companies. The companies paid him thousands of dollars for this right. The money went not to the government, but straight to Fall's bank account. The name of one piece of oil-rich land, Teapot Dome, soon was used to describe the crime, which became known as the Teapot Dome Scandal.

Charles Forbes, head of the Veterans Bureau, was arrested for selling government hospital supplies to private companies and keeping the profits for himself. Harding privately scolded Forbes, but he did not want to tell the public about the crime. Forbes resigned and left the country, and the president hoped the scandal would disappear before Americans learned about it. About two months later, another one of Harding's advisors killed himself. To make matters even worse, there were rumors that the president had a girlfriend. Sick with worry, Harding's health grew steadily weaker.

Harding and his cabinet in 1921. As Harding learned more about the corruption among his friends and advisors, he began to worry. "I have no trouble with my enemies," he once said. "But my friends … They're the ones that keep me walking the floor nights!"

DURING HARDING'S presidency, an Airedale terrier named Laddie Boy was his constant companion. The dog brought the newspaper to Harding every morning and even sat in on cabinet meetings in a special chair. When the president practiced golf on the White House lawn, Laddie Boy fetched the balls, scooping them up in his mouth and returning them for Harding's next shot. Newspaper columns were written about the dog. Many Americans wanted a pet just like the president's. A company named a canned food after him, and there was even a child's stuffed Laddie Boy toy.

At the dinner table in the White House dining room, Harding would offer treats from his plate to Laddie Boy. Mrs. Harding would tell the president to stop feeding the dog. Laddie Boy would then journey to her end of the table, where Mrs. Harding would feed him from her plate.

When the Hardings quarreled and weren't speaking, they shouted their communications to each other at the poor dog. "Laddie, tell the Duchess she's 100-percent wrong!"

29

Chapter FOUR

Journey to Disaster

In the summer of 1923, the Hardings left the capital to travel by train to the western United States. During the "Voyage of Understanding," Harding would give more than 80 speeches to admirers around the country and in Canada.

HARDING WAS TROUBLED BY THE CORRUPTION in his **administration.** It hurt him that people he believed were his friends had committed crimes. Harding wondered what to do. Should he tell the public what he knew? He asked his secretary of commerce, Herbert Hoover, for advice. Hoover suggested Harding tell newspaper reporters what he knew. At least that way, the American people would still believe that their president was an honest man.

Harding was too afraid to report the corruption. He decided it was a good time to leave Washington and planned a cross-country trip that would take him all the way to Alaska. Along the way, he would meet the people and give numerous speeches. He called this trip the "Voyage of Understanding"

because he planned to listen to the ideas and concerns of the American people.

President Harding was still ill. His blood pressure was high, and he often couldn't catch his breath. Just in case something should go wrong, the Hardings brought their doctor along for the journey. The president's train departed Washington on June 20, 1923.

The trip was a huge success, but the long journey was difficult for Harding. After reaching Alaska, the president's party took a boat down the West Coast to San Francisco. Along the way, Harding was struck by severe

The governor of Alaska wore a native parka made of fur when President and Mrs. Harding visited him in Anchorage. Harding's visit to Alaska was the first ever by a president.

stomach problems. By the time he reached the Palace Hotel in San Francisco, he had grown very weak.

On August 2, Mrs. Harding was reading to the president. Suddenly, he turned pale, saying he felt strange. Slowly, the color returned to his face, and Mrs. Harding continued to read. A few moments later, at 7:35 in the evening, Warren Harding was dead. The cause of his death was probably a heart attack. Vice President Calvin Coolidge was sworn in as president early the next morning.

Americans were struck with grief over Harding's death. Mourners lined the tracks as the train bearing Harding's body returned to Washington. His body lay in the White House East Room overnight. Mrs. Harding spent two hours sitting next to his casket talking to him. His body was then transferred to the Capitol, where thousands came to pay their respects. Finally, a train took Harding's remains back to Marion, Ohio, where he was buried. The president's widow died just 15 months later.

Unfortunately, news of the corruption in his administration began to reach the public after Harding's death. Stories about

his relationships with other women were reported in books and papers. Even worse, a few people even claimed that Mrs. Harding had murdered the president. She had refused to allow an **autopsy** on his body, which would have confirmed the cause of his death. Some people said she did this because she had killed him. New scandals surfaced as well, including the Teapot Dome Scandal. The president himself was not proven guilty of wrongdoing, but his good name suffered. The man who had been such a popular president quickly became known as a terrible leader. After all, it was his closest political friends that were guilty of the crimes.

Mourners waited in line for hours at the Capitol to pay their last respects to the president. Harding was still deeply loved by the nation's citizens. Unfortunately, news of the corruption in his administration would soon tarnish his name.

33

Harding had predicted that his "Voyage of Understanding" might be a mistake. Before he departed, he said the trip needed to be shortened or "it will kill me." Still, Harding couldn't resist the opportunity to meet the American people who so admired him.

In every list ranking the presidents from best to worst, Warren Harding has always been at the bottom. His presidency has been called "scandalous" and "corrupt." But during his lifetime, the American people loved him. Perhaps his biggest failure was not to reveal the corruption and try to stop it.

"I cannot hope to be one of the greatest presidents," Harding once said, "but perhaps I can be remembered as one of the best loved." Unfortunately, this was not to be. As much as Harding tried to be a good man, his presidency is remembered for its corruption.

WARREN HARDING'S FATHER, GEORGE (SHOWN BELOW), HAD LONG PRACTICED homeopathic medicine. This form of treating illness uses homemade treatments. George Harding believed that one could cure an illness by giving tiny doses of something that produces the same symptoms. How did George Harding treat a common cold? He made a medicine out of onions because they make the eyes water and the nose run.

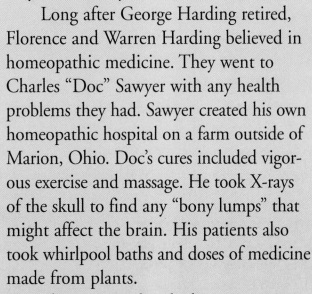

Long after George Harding retired, Florence and Warren Harding believed in homeopathic medicine. They went to Charles "Doc" Sawyer with any health problems they had. Sawyer created his own homeopathic hospital on a farm outside of Marion, Ohio. Doc's cures included vigorous exercise and massage. He took X-rays of the skull to find any "bony lumps" that might affect the brain. His patients also took whirlpool baths and doses of medicine made from plants.

Florence Harding had great trust in Doc's treatments. Sawyer even traveled with the Hardings to Alaska during the Voyage of Understanding. The president became ill with stomach problems just before he died, probably because of crabs he had eaten. Sawyer used medicine that caused diarrhea, claiming it would remove **"toxins"** from the body. Other doctors believed this treatment did more harm than good. They claimed the treatment might even have weakened Harding's heart, leading to a heart attack. No one knows for sure what caused Harding's death because an autopsy was never performed. But Florence stood by Doc Sawyer to the end.

35

1865 Warren Harding is born on November 2 in Corsica (now Blooming Grove), Ohio. His parents are George Tryon and Phoebe Dickerson Harding.

1873 The Harding family moves to Caledonia, Ohio, where George works as a homeopathic doctor. Phoebe earns money as a midwife. Warren takes his first job at the *Caledonia Argus* as a printer's devil.

1879 Harding enters Ohio Central College, where he edits the school newspaper and plays with a band. With the exception of high marks in spelling, his grades are not exceptional.

1882 Harding's family moves to Marion, Ohio. He takes a job at the Democratic weekly paper, the *Marion Democratic Mirror.*

1884 With two friends, Harding buys the *Marion Star,* a weekly newspaper. They publish the first edition on November 26.

1891 On July 8, Harding marries Florence Kling De Wolfe. She is five years older than he. Her father, Amos Kling, is the richest man in town. Mr. Kling objects to the marriage and refuses to attend the wedding.

1898 On November 6, Harding is elected an Ohio state senator. He meets Harry Daugherty, who will become a close political ally.

1903 Rewarded by the Republican Party for his loyalty, Harding is elected lieutenant governor of Ohio.

1910 Harding is defeated as the Republican candidate for governor.

1914 Harding is elected to the U.S. Senate. He will become an important figure in the Republican Party.

1917 Senator Harding votes in favor of prohibition, which makes the consumption of alcohol illegal in the United States.

1919 Harding votes in favor of women's suffrage. Prohibition becomes law when the 18th Amendment to the Constitution is approved.

1920 When the 19th Amendment is approved, American women are allowed to vote for the first time. Republicans open their national convention in Chicago on June 8 to nominate a presidential candidate. Harding is chosen. In August, he begins his "front-porch" campaign, speaking to supporters from his Marion, Ohio, home. He is elected president on November 2.

1921 Harding creates a cabinet made up of "great minds and old friends." Many of the "old friends" will later cause problems within his administration. Harding signs an act to establish the Bureau of the Budget. Harding helps create the Washington Conference for the Limitation of Armament.

1922 Albert Fall, Harding's secretary of the interior, leases oil reserves on government land to private oil companies on April 7. Harding makes the first presidential radio broadcast on June 14. He is the first president to speak on the radio.

1923 Charles Forbes, head of the Veterans Bureau, is accused of stealing hospital supplies and taking money from construction companies. On June 20, the Hardings begin a train trip across the country to Alaska, which the president calls his "Voyage of Understanding." The president delivers more than 80 speeches along the way. On July 26, Harding becomes the first president to visit Canada when he gives a speech in Vancouver, British Columbia. On July 28, Harding becomes ill from what his doctor calls food poisoning. On August 2, Warren Harding dies at 7:35 PM. He is 57 years old. Today most doctors believe the cause of his death was a heart attack. The next day, Vice President Calvin Coolidge is sworn in as president.

1924 Florence Harding dies on November 21, 15 months after her husband's death.

administration (ad-min-ih-STRAY-shun)
An administration is the group of people who are in charge of running the U.S. government. The president and his cabinet are the administration.

ambition (am-BISH-un)
Ambition is a strong desire to succeed. Florence Harding was full of ambition.

amendment (uh-MEND-ment)
An amendment is a change or addition made to the Constitution or other documents. The 19th Amendment gave American women the right to vote.

armament (AR-muh-ment)
Armament is weaponry and other equipment used by the military. Harding called a conference to reduce armament in countries around the world.

attorney general (uh-TUR-nee GEN-rul)
The attorney general is the chief lawyer of the country. Harding named Harry Daugherty the attorney general.

autopsy (AH-top-see)
An autopsy is a medical examination of a dead body usually done to determine the cause of death. An autopsy was never performed on Harding's body.

bills (BILZ)
Bills are ideas for new laws that are presented to a group of lawmakers. Harding proposed 132 bills during his time as a senator.

bureau (BYUR-oh)
A bureau is a division within a government department. Harding created the Bureau of the Budget.

cabinet (KAB-eh-net)
A cabinet is the group of people who advise a president. Harding chose many respected people for his cabinet, but he also chose some of his friends.

campaign (kam-PAYN)
A campaign is the process of running for an election, including activities such as giving speeches or attending rallies. Harding ran his campaign from his home in Ohio.

candidate (KAN-duh-det)
A candidate is a person running in an election. The Republicans chose Harding as their candidate for governor in 1910.

circulation (sur-kyoo-LAY-shun)
A newspaper's circulation is the number of copies it sells. Florence Harding took over the circulation department at the *Marion Star* and was in charge of making sure all the papers were delivered and paid for.

convention (kun-VEN-shun)
A convention is a meeting. The Democratic and Republican political parties hold national conventions every four years to choose their presidential candidates.

corruption (kuh-RUP-shun)
Corruption is dishonesty. Harding's friends were accused of corruption.

creed (KREED)
A creed is a statement of beliefs by which to live. Harding created a creed for his employees at the *Marion Star* to follow.

delegates (DEL-eh-gitz)
Delegates are people elected to take part in something. Delegates at the Republican National Convention chose Harding as their 1920 presidential candidate.

Democrat (DEM-uh-crat)
A Democrat is a member of the Democratic Party, one of the two major political parties in the United States. The Democrats are opponents of the Republicans.

editorials (ed-ih-TOR-ee-ulz)
Editorials are articles that give the opinion of the editor or publisher of a newspaper. Warren Harding wrote editorials for the *Marion Star.*

homeopathic (hom-ee-oh-PATH-ik)
Homeopathic medicine is a kind of medical practice that treats an illness with small doses of medicine that produce symptoms of the illness. George Harding was a homeopathic doctor.

journalism (JER-nl-iz-um)
Journalism is the work of gathering, writing, and presenting truthful stories for newspapers and magazines (or for television and radio). Harding liked the idea of working in journalism and seeing his words in print.

landslide (LAND-slyd)
If a candidate wins an election by a landslide, he or she wins by a huge number of votes. Harding won the 1920 presidential election by a landslide.

nominate (NOM-ih-nayt)
If a political party nominates some-one, it chooses him or her to run for a political office. Harding worried that he might be nominated as the Republican presidential candidate.

policies (PAWL-uh-seez)
Policies are rules made to help run a government or other organization. Harding always went along with Republican Party policies.

**political parties
(puh-LIT-uh-kul PAR-teez)**
Political parties are groups of people who share similar ideas about how to run a government. People from opposing political parties often have differences of opinion.

politics (PAWL-uh-tiks)
Politics refers to the actions and practices of the government. Harding did not think he was cut out for a life in politics.

rally (RAL-ee)
A rally is an organized gathering of people to show support for something or someone. Harding went to a Republican rally in 1884 to support a candidate.

Republicans (ree-PUB-leh-kunz)
Republicans are members of the Republican Party, one of the two major political parties in the United States. Warren Harding was a Republican.

scandal (SKAN-dul)
A scandal is a shameful action that shocks the public. Harding hoped the scandals involving his friends would disappear before Americans found out about them.

secretary of the interior (SEK-ruh-tayr-ee of the in-TEER-ee-ur)
The secretary of the interior is a member of the president's cabinet. He or she heads the department in charge of how U.S. land is used.

sensational (sen-SAY-shun-ul)
If a newspaper article is sensational, it is meant to stir up strong feelings in its readers. Harding hated sensational stories filled with crime, tragedy, and misfortune.

treasury (TREZH-ur-ee)
A treasury manages the flow of money in a government, including its income and expenses. Andrew Mellon was Harding's secretary of the treasury.

tuition (too-ISH-un)
Tuition is a fee for attending a school. Harding used the extra money he earned painting barns to help pay his college tuition.

toxins (TOK-sinz)
Toxins are poisons of any kind that have a bad effect on human health. A doctor thought that crabs Harding ate had infected the president's body with toxins.

Our PRESENTS

Our PRESIDENTS

President	Birthplace	Life Span	Presidency	Political Party	First Lady
George Washington	Virginia	1732–1799	1789–1797	None	Martha Dandridge Custis Washington
John Adams	Massachusetts	1735–1826	1797–1801	Federalist	Abigail Smith Adams
Thomas Jefferson	Virginia	1743–1826	1801–1809	Democratic-Republican	widower
James Madison	Virginia	1751–1836	1809–1817	Democratic Republican	Dolley Payne Todd Madison
James Monroe	Virginia	1758–1831	1817–1825	Democratic Republican	Elizabeth Kortright Monroe
John Quincy Adams	Massachusetts	1767–1848	1825–1829	Democratic-Republican	Louisa Johnson Adams
Andrew Jackson	South Carolina	1767–1845	1829–1837	Democrat	widower
Martin Van Buren	New York	1782–1862	1837–1841	Democrat	widower
William H. Harrison	Virginia	1773–1841	1841	Whig	Anna Symmes Harrison
John Tyler	Virginia	1790–1862	1841–1845	Whig	Letitia Christian Tyler / Julia Gardiner Tyler
James K. Polk	North Carolina	1795–1849	1845–1849	Democrat	Sarah Childress Polk

Our PRESIDENTS

President	Birthplace	Life Span	Presidency	Political Party	First Lady
Zachary Taylor	Virginia	1784–1850	1849–1850	Whig	Margaret Mackall Smith Taylor
Millard Fillmore	New York	1800–1874	1850–1853	Whig	Abigail Powers Fillmore
Franklin Pierce	New Hampshire	1804–1869	1853–1857	Democrat	Jane Means Appleton Pierce
James Buchanan	Pennsylvania	1791–1868	1857–1861	Democrat	never married
Abraham Lincoln	Kentucky	1809–1865	1861–1865	Republican	Mary Todd Lincoln
Andrew Johnson	North Carolina	1808–1875	1865–1869	Democrat	Eliza McCardle Johnson
Ulysses S. Grant	Ohio	1822–1885	1869–1877	Republican	Julia Dent Grant
Rutherford B. Hayes	Ohio	1822–1893	1877–1881	Republican	Lucy Webb Hayes
James A. Garfield	Ohio	1831–1881	1881	Republican	Lucretia Rudolph Garfield
Chester A. Arthur	Vermont	1829–1886	1881–1885	Republican	widower
Grover Cleveland	New Jersey	1837–1908	1885–1889	Democrat	Frances Folsom Cleveland

Our PRESIDENTS

President	Birthplace	Life Span	Presidency	Political Party	First Lady
Benjamin Harrison	Ohio	1833–1901	1889–1893	Republican	Caroline Scott Harrison
Grover Cleveland	New Jersey	1837–1908	1893–1897	Democrat	Frances Folsom Cleveland
William McKinley	Ohio	1843–1901	1897–1901	Republican	Ida Saxton McKinley
Theodore Roosevelt	New York	1858–1919	1901–1909	Republican	Edith Kermit Carow Roosevelt
William H. Taft	Ohio	1857–1930	1909–1913	Republican	Helen Herron Taft
Woodrow Wilson	Virginia	1856–1924	1913–1921	Democrat	Ellen L. Axson Wilson Edith Bolling Galt Wilson
Warren G. Harding	Ohio	1865–1923	1921–1923	Republican	Florence Kling De Wolfe Harding
Calvin Coolidge	Vermont	1872–1933	1923–1929	Republican	Grace Goodhue Coolidge
Herbert C. Hoover	Iowa	1874–1964	1929–1933	Republican	Lou Henry Hoover
Franklin D. Roosevelt	New York	1882–1945	1933–1945	Democrat	Anna Eleanor Roosevelt Roosevelt
Harry S. Truman	Missouri	1884–1972	1945–1953	Democrat	Elizabeth Wallace Truman

Our PRESIDENTS

President	Birthplace	Life Span	Presidency	Political Party	First Lady
Dwight D. Eisenhower	Texas	1890–1969	1953–1961	Republican	Mary "Mamie" Doud Eisenhower
John F. Kennedy	Massachusetts	1917–1963	1961–1963	Democrat	Jacqueline Bouvier Kennedy
Lyndon B. Johnson	Texas	1908–1973	1963–1969	Democrat	Claudia Alta Taylor Johnson
Richard M. Nixon	California	1913–1994	1969–1974	Republican	Thelma Catherine Ryan Nixon
Gerald Ford	Nebraska	1913–	1974–1977	Republican	Elizabeth "Betty" Bloomer Warren Ford
James Carter	Georgia	1924–	1977–1981	Democrat	Rosalynn Smith Carter
Ronald Reagan	Illinois	1911–	1981–1989	Republican	Nancy Davis Reagan
George Bush	Massachusetts	1924–	1989–1993	Republican	Barbara Pierce Bush
William Clinton	Arkansas	1946–	1993–2001	Democrat	Hillary Rodham Clinton
George W. Bush	Connecticut	1946–	2001–	Republican	Laura Welch Bush

Presidential FACTS

Qualifications

To run for president, a candidate must

- be at least 35 years old
- be a citizen who was born in the United States
- have lived in the United States for 14 years

Term of Office

A president's term of office is four years. No president can stay in office for more than two terms.

Election Date

The presidential election takes place every four years on the first Tuesday of November.

Inauguration Date

Presidents are inaugurated on January 20.

Oath of Office

I do solemnly swear I will faithfully execute the office of the President of the United States and will to the best of my ability preserve, protect, and defend the Constitution of the United States.

Write a Letter to the President

One of the best things about being a U.S. citizen is that Americans get to participate in their government. They can speak out if they feel government leaders aren't doing their jobs. They can also praise leaders who are going the extra mile. Do you have something you'd like the president to do? Should the president worry more about the environment and encourage people to recycle? Should the government spend more money on our schools? You can write a letter to the president to say how you feel!

1600 Pennsylvania Avenue
Washington, D.C. 20500

You can even send an e-mail to: president@whitehouse.gov

Internet Sites

Learn more about Warren Harding and other presidents from Ohio:
http://homepages.rootsweb.com/~maggieoh/Pres/pres.htm

Visit the Warren Harding home in Marion, Ohio:
http://www.ohiohistory.org/places/harding/index.html

Learn more about Harding's trip to Alaska:
http://www.mosquitonet.com/~ranchmotel/harding.html

Learn more about the 18th Amendment (prohibition):
http://www.history.ohio-state.edu/projects/prohibition/default.htm

Learn more about the 19th Amendment (women's suffrage):
http://lcweb2.loc.gov/ammem/vfwhtml/vfwhome.html
http://www.nmwh.org/exhibits/exhibit_frames.html

Learn more about the Teapot Dome Scandal:
http://www.gi.grolier.com/presidents/aae/side/teapot.html

Learn more about all the presidents and visit the White House:
http://www.whitehouse.gov/WH/glimpse/presidents/html/presidents.html
http://www.thepresidency.org/presinfo.htm
http://www.americanpresidents.org/

Books

Cohen, Daniel. *Prohibition: America Makes Alcohol Illegal* (Spotlight on American History). Brookfield, CT: Millbrook Press, 1995.

Dolan, Edward. *America in World War I.* Brookfield, CT: Millbrook Press, 1996.

Granfield, Linda. *Extra! Extra!: The Who, What, Where, When, and Why of Newspapers.* New York: Orchard Books, 1994.

Monroe, Judy. *The Nineteenth Amendment: Women's Right to Vote.* Springfield, NJ: Enslow Publishers, 1998.

Schraff, Anne. *Woodrow Wilson* (United States Presidents). Springfield, NJ: Enslow Publishers, 1998.

Index

alcohol, prohibition on, 18, 36-37
automobiles, 22, 25

barter system, 6
Blaine, James G., 9
Bureau of Budget, 24-25, 37

Cleveland, Grover, 9
Coolidge, Calvin, 23, 32
corruption, 27-28, 30, 32-34
Cox, James, 17

Daugherty, Harry, 23, 36
De Wolfe, Florence Kling. *See* Harding, Florence

18th Amendment, 18, 37

Fall, Albert, 22-23, 27, 37
Forbes, Charles, 23, 28, 37
front-porch campaign, 20-21

Harding, Florence, 12-16, 18, 33, 35-36
  death of, 37
  health problems, 18, 27
  social life of, 27
  support for women's suffrage, 19
  on Voyage of Understanding, 31-32
Harding, George Tryon, 6-9, 35-36
Harding, Phoebe Dickerson, 6-8, 36
Harding, Warren G.
  birth of, 6, 36
  cabinet of, 22, 27-28, 37
  campaign for Ohio governorship, 16, 36
  death of, 32, 35, 37
  education of, 7-9, 36
  election of, 21, 37
  health problems of, 18, 27, 28, 31-33
  journalism career, 8-14, 36
  as lieutenant governor, 15, 36
  at *Marion Democratic Mirror,* 9, 36
  marriage of, 13, 36
  as Ohio senator, 15, 36
  as owner of *Marion Star,* 10-11, 14, 36
  popularity of, 8, 21
  presidential campaign, 20-21, 37
  presidential nomination, 17-18, 37
  presidential term, 22-30

  ranking of, 34
  rumors about, 28, 32-33
  social life, 27
  as U.S. senator, 16-17, 36
Harding Publishing Company, 14
Herrick, Myron T., 15
highway construction, 25
homeopathic medicine, 35
Hoover, Herbert, 22, 30
Hughes, Charles Evans, 22

Kling, Amos, 12, 14, 36

Laddie Boy, 29, 34
League of Nations, 22, 37
Lowden, Frank O., 17

Marion Star, 10, 14-15, 36
  creed of, 10, 11
Mellon, Andrew, 22

19th Amendment, 19, 37

prohibition, 18, 36-37

Return to Normalcy campaign theme, 20
Roosevelt, Franklin D., 17
Ruth, Babe, 25

Sawyer, Charles "Doc," 35
scandals, 27-28
steel companies, 32
suffragettes, 19

taxes, 25

Teapot Dome Scandal, 27-28, 33
technological inventions, 23-24, 27, 32
typesetting process, 9

Vancouver, British Columbia, 32, 37
Voyage of Understanding, 30-31, 34-35, 37

Washington Conference for the Limitation of
  Armament, 26, 37
White House, 27
Wilson, Woodrow, 17, 20, 22, 36
women's suffrage, 19, 37
Wood, Leonard, 17